A
WORKSHOP
ON

The Book of Job

Finding Comfort and Purpose in Suffering

DIANE BRUMMEL BLOEM

Lamplighter Books Grand Rapids, Michigan
Zondervan Publishing House

This book is dedicated to all the Christian school teachers and Sunday school teachers whose loving training by word and example has inspired me and encouraged me to live for the Lord.

Books in the Workshop Series

A Workshop on Self-Giving
  by Marilyn Anderes

A Workshop on Bible Marriages
  by Diane Brummel Bloem with Robert C. Bloem

A Workshop on the Beatitudes
  by Diane Brummel Bloem

A Workshop on the Book of Proverbs
  by Diane Brummel Bloem

A Workshop on the Book of Colossians
  by Margaret and Paul Fromer

A Workshop on the Book of Philippians
  by Margaret and Paul Fromer

A Workshop on the Book of John
  by Carolyn Nystrom

A Workshop on the Book of Romans
  by Carolyn Nystrom

A Workshop on the Christian Faith
  by Carolyn Nystrom

A Workshop on David and His Psalms
  by Carolyn Nystrom

A Workshop on the Book of James
  by Carolyn Nystrom and Margaret Fromer

A Workshop on Time Management
  by Ann Roecker

I will extol the LORD at all times;
  his praise will always be on my lips.
My soul will boast in the LORD;
  let the afflicted hear and rejoice.
Glorify the LORD with me;
  let us exalt his name together.
I sought the LORD, and he answered me;
  he delivered me from all my fears.
Those who look to him are radiant;
  their faces are never covered with shame.

The righteous cry out, and the LORD hears them;
  he delivers them from all their troubles.
The LORD is close to the brokenhearted
  and saves those who are crushed in spirit.

The LORD redeems his servants;
  no one who takes refuge in him will be
    condemned.
                    Psalm 34:1–5, 17–18, 22

CONTENTS

Preface 9
Acknowledgments 13
Explanatory Notes 15
1. Introducing Job—His First Test 17
    Job 1
2. Job's Second Test 21
    Job 2–3
3. Eliphaz Speaks and Job Replies 24
    Job 4-7
4. Bildad's Speech and Job's Reply 29
    Job 8–10
5. Zophar Talks and Job Answers 34
    Job 11–14
6. Eliphaz Attacks Again and Job Responds 38
    Job 15–17

7. Bildad and Zophar Speak Again and Job
   Answers 42
      Job 18–21
8. Eliphaz and Job Exchange Words 48
      Job 22–24
9. Bildad and Job Exchange Words 53
      Job 25-31
10. Elihu Gives Youthful Advice 59
      Job 32–37
11. God Speaks 65
      Job 38–39
12. God Continues 68
      Job 40–41
13. Job Is Restored 72
      Job 42
Bibliography 77

PREFACE

"Is this year's study of Job going to be depressing?" asked Joann. "I like to come home from Bible study feeling I've been lifted."

"Joann, I've never studied anything so interesting!" I answered. "This is, as you suspect, a book about intense suffering. It's also about God's majesty and sovereignty and our hope for eternal life. It probes the deep questions of God's dealing with humans and studies how people react and interact in times of great trial. You will be lifted and challenged and comforted!"

*   *   *

Many times I have tried to find just the right words to say to some suffering person. I've wanted to put a Band-Aid of words on the hurt and move on, not really understanding the agony of the sufferer and of his or her loved ones. Then, in one year, God taught me many lessons.

In January, 1981, a call informed us that my mother-in-law was lying in bed and could not speak. She had suffered a massive stroke and remained in a coma in intensive care for three long weeks before dying. During this time my mother developed severe heart problems and was brought to that same intensive care unit.

About two weeks later, in February, my father slipped and fractured his spine. We learned that it fractured so readily and was so painful because he had bone cancer. In March my father-in-law had major surgery and afterwards was so weak and confused he had to move to a nursing home.

In June our son was married in a ceremony we could not attend because he was 2,000 miles away and my father was so ill. In October my father, wasted by disease and pain but confident of his salvation, went to heaven.

The year 1982 brought more testing. My mother decided to move to a retirement home, so we sold her home, disbursed many of her things, and helped her make the adjustment. In June she became desperately ill with meningitis but after several weeks began to recover. Meanwhile my father-in-law continued to slowly lose strength. In November I discovered a lump in my breast and faced the agony of a possible diagnosis of cancer. Praise God the tumor was benign!

* * *

Before 1981 I had had little trouble in my life. I made plans, and most of the time things worked out the way I hoped and prayed they would. The Book of Job didn't mean much to me. Without realizing it or intending it, I sometimes said painful things to people who suffered in trials.

But through my own trials God opened my eyes. I met

many sufferers and their families. I learned that there are highs and lows in suffering—sometimes the trial makes one feel so close to God the experience becomes ecstatic joy, but on other days depression, doubt, and death crush one to a pulp. I felt that the trials separated me from the "normal" lives of my friends, yet I found joy in their expressions of love. I felt close to others who were tested by God.

In 1981 and 1982 I studied the Psalms with the three study groups I led. As we learned about the sufferings and joys of the psalmists and found that we had similar experiences, we often turned to the Book of Job for answers. We saw that God's people throughout the ages have had similar experiences. Consequently this book combines the study of Job with many references to the Psalms and experiences of other believers recorded in the Bible.

Near the end of his life, my father said his comfort was found in Psalm 46:10, "Be still, and know that I am God." I pray and trust that this study will bring you that blessed assurance and that your faith may be strengthened.

Diane Brummel Bloem

ACKNOWLEDGMENTS

I thank Reverend Leonard Greenway, Th.M., Th.D., for suggesting, encouraging, and evaluating this study.

I thank the two hundred women and men in the four groups I led in this study for their faithful work, perceptive questions and comments, and their candid criticisms. The thoughts and experiences they shared with me have fleshed out this work, and their puzzled looks and kind comments have removed many flaws.

I thank my husband, Robert C. Bloem, and our children for listening to me talk things through and for studying and learning with me.

Most of all I thank God for hearing and answering my constant prayer:

"O teach me, Lord, that I may teach
The precious things thou dost impart
And wing my words that they may reach
The hidden depths of many a heart."

EXPLANATORY NOTES

Many questions are asked—by man and by God—in the Book of Job. These questions are teaching tools. They involve both the questioner and those addressed in a search for truth.

This study also involves questions. They are essential in involving the leader and the students in the search for truth. Some questions have obvious answers, some involve more thought, some require an answer from personal experience. Those who have studied these lessons with me found some of the questions difficult but the search for an answer rewarding. It is essential that each person attempt to answer each question in advance so that the group discussion is rich and meaningful, securely based on God's Word.

Themes are repeated in the book of Job and therefore are repeated in this study too. This repetition develops understanding and reinforces truths. Though some ideas and problems recur, the approach or answer changes, and each lesson applies the material in new ways.

I have met many "Jobs" in this year of study. They are present throughout the Bible and in contemporary life. Lest Job seem to be an isolated case, many other Bible passages are referred to for perspective.

If your schedule does not permit thirteen meetings for discussion, lessons 11 and 12 may be combined, or lesson 10 may be omitted.

"Man" and "mankind" are often used generically in this book. No discrimination against women is intended.

I have quoted from the New International Version (NIV), but I have also consulted the Revised Standard Version (RSV), the King James Version (KJV), the New English Bible (NEB), and the American Standard Version (ASV).

1

INTRODUCING JOB—HIS FIRST TEST

Job 1

Job's story is thought to take place at the time of the patriarchs—Abraham, Isaac, and Jacob—about 2,000 years before Christ was born. Clues that point to this timing are the roving Sabean and Chaldean tribes (1:15, 17); Job's wealth being measured by the number of animals he possessed; and Job's lifestyle, which was similar to Abraham's but not typically Israelitish.

No one knows where the land of Uz, where Job lived, was. We do know Uz was a son of Aram, who was a son of Shem (Gen. 10:21–23), and there are many Aramaic qualities in the Book of Job. Aramaic tribes lived in northern Mesopotamia and on the borders of Babylonia and Palestine.

Several manuscripts from early civilizations deal with the topic of suffering and have similarities to the biblical account of Job. Since earliest civilization, humans have wrestled with the problem of suffering—especially suffering borne by exemplary moral people.

> [But] Job stands far above its nearest competitors, in the coherence of its sustained treatment of the theme of human misery, in the scope of its many-sided examination of the problem, in the strength and clarity of its defiant moral monotheism, in the characterization of the protagonists, in the heights of its lyrical poetry, in its dramatic impact, and in the intellectual integrity with which it faces the "unintelligible burden" of human existence. In all this Job stands alone. Nothing we know before it provided a model, and nothing since, including its numerous imitations, has risen to the same heights. Comparison only serves to enhance the solitary greatness of the book of Job.*

Job is acknowledged to be wisdom literature, poetry, and drama.

> The book of Job is an astonishing mixture of almost every kind of literature to be found in the Old Testament. Many individual pieces can be isolated and identified as proverbs, riddles, hymns, laments, curses, lyrical nature poems.†

The Holy Spirit inspired the author of Job to write about a believer in the one true God—a believer who challenges the justice of his personal God. This challenge provides God with the vehicle to reveal Himself, His power, His personal concern, and His control of the believer's life. This book has been acknowledged for thousands of years as inspired by God for the teaching of His children.

Note: One must be careful when using verses from Job to prove a point; the context should be carefully noted. Much of what Job's friends said was true. We even find Paul quoting

---

*Francis I. Anderson, Job: An Introduction and Commentary (Downers Grove, Illinois: Inter-Varsity Press, 1976), p. 32.

†Ibid., p. 33.

Eliphaz to the Corinthians (see Job 5:13 and 1 Cor. 3:19). Yet Job's friends often distorted the truth as they attempted to apply it to Job, and they are rebuked by God.

JOB 1

1. Describe the person Job, using verses 1–5. _____

_____

_____

_____

2. Describe Job's family. _____

_____

_____

_____

3. How was Job like Christian parents today? _____

_____

_____

4. Satan says, "Does Job fear God for nothing?" (1:9). Do we fear and honor God because of what we get from Him?

_____

Is that a good motive? Explain. _____

_____

_____

5. Why is God so confident Job could stand severe testing?

_____

_____

Can God say the same about you? _____

6. a. What frightens you in verses 6–12? _____

_____

_____

_____

b. What comforts you? _____

_____

_____

7. Job's first test is to lose all his material possessions and his family. What was his reaction (verse 20)? _____

_____

_____

8. Rephrase verse 21 in your own words. _____

_____

_____

9. What does it mean to charge God with wrongdoing (1:22)? _____

_____

Do we ever do that? _____

10. How would you react if you lost your family and all your material possessions? _____

_____

What would comfort you? _____

_____

2

JOB'S SECOND TEST

Job 2–3

Job lost his children and all his material possessions, but he still had his wife, his friends, and most important, his health. Now Satan proposes the ultimate test.

JOB 2

1. a. What was Satan's reply to God's question (verses 1–2)? _____

_____

b. What had Satan been doing (1 Peter 5:8)?_____

_____

2. Do you agree with Satan's words in verses 4 and 5? Explain. _____

_____

_____

3. Why does God sometimes allow Satan to test us? See James 1:2–4, 12. _____

_____

4. a. Was Job's wife being tested too (verse 9)? _____ How did she react to these troubles? _____

_____

b. Was Job's answer helpful to her (verse 10)? Explain.

_____

5. a. In what ways do other family members suffer when one of them is stricken by accident or disease (if one has cancer, is badly burned, is paralyzed, or becomes extremely depressed or confused)?_____

_____

_____

b. What will comfort and help family members? _____

_____

6. How can the afflicted person help his or her family members? _____

_____

7. a. What did Job's friends decide to do (verse 11)? _____

_____

b. What was their reaction (verses 12–13)? _____

_____

_____

c. Did this comfort Job? _____

_____

8. Does it help to have friends with you when you are in agony? Explain. _____

_____

9. Share some experiences in which you have been blessed by Christian friends when you were undergoing trials.

JOB 3

10. What questions does Job ask in this chapter? _____

_____

_____

11. a. Was it wrong for Job to curse his birth or wish he could die? Explain. _____

_____

_____

b. Did he consider suicide? _____

_____

12. In discussing Job 1:10, we were comforted that God placed an impenetrable hedge around the believer. Did Job find any comfort in being hedged in by God (3:23)? Explain.

_____

_____

13. a. Read Psalm 88 as if Job wrote it.

b. Pray for people who are suffering and calling out to God.

3

ELIPHAZ SPEAKS AND JOB REPLIES

Job 4–7

Job's friend Eliphaz (ĕĺ e făz) the Temanite may have been the great-grandson of Esau, or at least one of his descendants, and as such might have been taught to know the true God. We gather this after reading in Genesis 36:10–11, 15 that Esau and his wife Adah had a son whose name was Eliphaz. The oldest son of Eliphaz was Teman, who became a chief in the land of Edom.

The prophet Jeremiah speaks of Teman as an area of Edom known for its wise people, "Concerning Edom: This is what the Lord Almighty says: 'Is there no longer wisdom in Teman? Has counsel perished from the prudent? Has their wisdom decayed?' " (Jer. 49:7).

Eliphaz may have been the oldest of the friends because he speaks first. He is touched by Job's suffering and believes he can help his friend.

JOB 4

1. What is the tone of verses 2—6? _____

_____

Note: The key to Eliphaz's speech lies imbedded in a tribute to God's power. The summary of his belief is found in verses 7 and 8, which can be restated as, "If you suffer, you must have sinned. This is punishment you deserve from God."

2. Do you agree with Eliphaz that if people are having trouble, they must have caused trouble (Job 4:8)? _____

_____

3. In verses 12—21 Eliphaz tells about a dream he had. What is the message of the dream and to whom is it directed?

_____

_____

_____

Note: Verse 18 is considered very difficult to translate. It may refer to Satan and his fallen angels, who roam the world tempting people.

JOB 5

4. In a roundabout way, what is Eliphaz accusing Job of in verses 1—4? _____

_____

5. a. What does Eliphaz tell Job to do in verse 8? Why (verses 9—16)? _____

_____

_____

_____

b. Have you ever expressed these thoughts to a suffering person? _____

_____

6. Are the thoughts in verses 17–27 comforting? Why or why not? _____

_____

_____

JOB 6

7. We often speak of trials and temptations as a unit (James 1:2–18). What temptations come to people who suffer severe trials? _____

_____

8. What does Job hope for (verses 1–10)? Why? _____

_____

_____

Note: Job, who is known for his patience, says that it is difficult to be patient when one has no hope (6:11).

9. Read verse 14. How should Christians treat someone who, in deep despair, denies his or her faith? _____

_____

_____

10. How were Job's friends like a stream of water (verses 15–21)? _____

_____

11. In verse 21 Job observes a fact also true today: people often turn away from handicapped, disfigured, or suffering people. Why is this true? _____

_____

_____

Note: In verses 22–23 Job is saying, "I didn't ask for money. All I wanted was friendship."

12. Give examples of times when the words of suffering persons are not regarded as having "weight" or significance (see 6:26). _____

_____

Note: Verse 27 is almost an insult-exchange. Job feels insulted because Eliphaz believes Job is being punished for his sins. Job retaliates by saying, "You are so heartless that you would even gamble over an orphan or a friend." He speaks of a callousness like that displayed by the soldiers who gambled for Jesus' robe as He was dying on the cross.

JOB 7

13. a. Why do nights seem so long when one is suffering (verses 1–4, 13–14)? _____

_____

_____

   b. What comforts you in such a situation? _____

_____

14. Explain Job's deep depression in verses 5–16. _____

_____

_____

15. a. To whom is Job speaking in verses 17–21? _____

_____

b. Contrast these verses with Psalm 8:3–9. Why is the emphasis so different? _____

_____

16. What special truth has the Holy Spirit taught you in this lesson? _____

_____

_____

CONCLUSION

Job's friends disappointed him. Jesus is the Friend who never fails. He stays with us through experiences that no one else can understand or share.

4

BILDAD'S SPEECH AND JOB'S REPLY

Job 8–10

In Job 6:26, Job said, "Do you mean to correct what I say, and treat the words of a despairing man as wind?" Were Bildad's ears closed, or wasn't he present when Job gave this heart-rending reply to Eliphaz? Bildad begins his speech by calling Job a windbag (Job 8:2). Yet as Job's friend, he tries to help by warning him.

Bildad may have been an Aramean descendant of Abraham and a descendant of Keturah's son Shuah (Gen. 25:2, 6). He may have been Job's age—fairly young (Job 8:8–9).

JOB 8

1. How do you suppose Job reacted to Bildad's statement that Job's children were killed because of their sin (verse 4)?

2. Even if Job's children did die as punishment for their sin, Job's resulting grief was not punishment for *his* sin, as Bildad implied. When someone sins and suffers the consequences, many people suffer with such a person.

For example, if a child becomes addicted to drugs and his or her body and life deteriorate, parents of such a person also suffer. Or if someone rapes or robs, that person may waste away in prison, but the innocent victim also suffers severely.

Again and again in the study of Job we are faced with the question, Is suffering punishment from God, or is it loving discipline (chastisement)?

Read each of the following Bible passages: Proverbs 3:11–12; Hebrews 12:5–11; Revelation 3:19; 2 Thessalonians 1:8–9; Romans 8:1–4; 3:21–26. Is suffering ever punishment for a born-again Christian? _____

What is the difference between punishment and discipline? _____

_____

Note: We have talked about the "cause-and-effect theology" of Job's friends. Verse 6 is an example of this. Bildad calls for Job to change his behavior, which would cause God to change His behavior toward Job.

3. Bildad bolsters his arguments by referring Job to the wisdom of the ancients—philosophers of long ago or older people who have lived and learned through many experiences (Job 8:8–10). Are older people better comforters than younger people? Why or why not? Consider Psalm 71:14–24. _____

_____

4. How would you respond to Bildad's statement in verse 20? _____

_____

5. What is the tone of Bildad's speech? _____

_____

6. What is the main message of his speech? _____

_____

JOB 9

7. How does Job respond to the tone of Bildad's speech?

_____

8. a. What were Job and the psalmist struggling with (Job 9:2; Ps. 49:7–9)? _____

_____

b. What was the Old Testament answer to their question? See Psalm 119:41–48. _____

_____

c. What is your answer? See Romans 3:21–26. _____

_____

9. Compare Job's statements in 1:21–22 with his words in 9:11–19. How has his reaction changed? _____

_____

_____

10. Job accuses God in verses 21–24 of being unjust. Do you agree that God does not seem to care about justice? Consider Isaiah 10:1–4. _____

_____

Note: Many commentators say that 9:25—35 are spoken to God. It seems to me that Job continues to speak to his friends saying that no matter what he says or does (verse 27), they have prejudged him (verse 22) and will portray him as a filthy sinner (verses 30—31).

11. What does Job long for in verses 32—35? _____

What is the answer to that longing? See Hebrews 7:24—25.

_____

_____

JOB 10

Job is so bitter and miserable he doesn't care if he dies, yet he wants to be free from God's condemnation.

12. What is Job saying to God in Job 10:3, 8—9? _____

_____

_____

13. Do you believe that God is like the Gestapo or secret police, watching us suspiciously, hoping to catch us in sin so He can punish us (10:13—17)? _____

_____

14. Is it wrong to ask God, "Why?" or "Why me?"? Consult Job 10:3—8, 18; Psalms 74:1, 10—11; 88:14; 89:46; Matthew 27:46. _____

_____

_____

_____

15. God gives *some* answers to our questions. Find three purposes for suffering in 2 Corinthians 1:3—11. _____

CONCLUSION

Job had his ups and downs. One moment he recognized God's power and questioned Him in faith. The next moment he fell into deep depression. He ended his speech in gloom, wishing he had not been born. He did not, however, see death as a wonderful alternative; he described it as "gloom," "deep shadow," "deepest night," "disorder," and "darkness" (verses 18–22). He wants to hide from God.

We too have our ups and downs. We feel the pressure of God's hand upon us. Sometimes we want to hide from Him. It's a good thing we can't get away from God because separation from Him is hell. Read Psalm 139:5–12, 23–24.

5

ZOPHAR TALKS AND JOB ANSWERS

Job 11—14

In these chapters we meet Job's third friend, Zophar. We know little about him except that he came from Naamah, and nobody knows for sure where that was. Zophar listened quietly to five long speeches. Now the tension building in him snaps, and he slings harsh words at Job. He doesn't want to hear about Job's righteousness.

JOB 11

1. a. Zophar, probably referring to Job's words in chapter 10, rebukes him for talking so personally to God—as man to man. He considers this evidence that Job is not blameless. Was it wrong for Job to talk to God this intimately? _____

_____

b. Why do people today sometimes rebuke believers for praying this way? _____

_____

2. a. How did Zophar expect his words, "Know this: God has even forgotten some of your sin" to comfort Job (verse 6b)? _____

_____

    b. Compare his words to those of the psalmist in Psalm 103:3−4, 8−12. _____

_____

Note: In Job 11:7−11 Zophar reverently tells of the incomprehensibility of God. Realizing this, however, does not prevent him from assuming the role of God's spokesman.

3. a. How does Zophar insult Job in 11:12? _____

_____

    b. What is Job's sarcastic answer (12:1−3)? _____

_____

4. If a person lives according to Zophar's advice in 11:13−19, will he or she be secure and trouble free? Explain.

_____

_____

5. What do you think of Zophar after reading his speech?

_____

JOB 12

Job fights back with sarcasm. Notice that most of these speeches begin heatedly and then calm down. Also be aware that Job uses plural pronouns. He is answering all three friends.

6. Do people who prosper and have smooth lives despise or have contempt for those who experience hard times (verse 5)? For example, in a time of depression and unemployment, are most employed, successful people truly sympathetic to the unemployed? Explain. _____

_____

_____

7. a. Is it true, as Job says in verse 6, that criminals and idolaters don't have troubles? _____

_____

b. What is the psalmist's answer to this problem in Psalm 73? _____

_____

c. Why did the psalmist have these feelings (Ps. 73:21)?

_____

d. Is this also true of Job? _____

8. How does Job comfort himself with the words in verses 7–25? _____

_____

_____

_____

JOB 13

In verse 3 Job turns from his friends and wants to speak directly with God. We know that God welcomes this because we read in Isaiah 1:18, " 'Come now, let us reason together,' says the LORD."

9. What can we learn from verses 4–5 about comforting those who suffer? _____

_____

_____

10. Compare verses 6—12 with Matthew 7:1—5. What is the message here? _____

_____

_____

11. a. Compare Job's boldness in coming into God's holy, royal presence (verses 14—16) to Esther's predicament in Esther 4:10—11, 15—16. Who was in greater danger—Job or Esther? Why? _____

_____

_____

b. What is Job's hope (verses 16 and 18)? _____

_____

c. Did Mordecai have this same hope (Esther 4:12—14)?

12. Does Job claim to be sinless (verses 20—27)? _____

Note: The imagery (words that create pictures in our minds) in verses 26 and 27 is vivid. In verse 26 Job says God is like a doctor writing out a prescription—making him take bitter medicine. In verse 27 he says he is hobbled, and God is tracking him much as a detective follows footprints or boot treadmarks when tracking criminals.

13. Read Psalm 38. How is David's experience like Job's?

_____

JOB 14

14. Describe and explain Job's mood in this chapter. _____

_____

15. What is Job depending on in his statement of faith in verses 14—17? _____

_____

_____

6

ELIPHAZ ATTACKS AGAIN AND JOB RESPONDS

Job 15–17

Again Eliphaz speaks. He asks several rhetorical questions, implying that Job's irreverent words are wind—empty claims to wisdom and righteousness. He calls Job a windbag.

Job replies in kind, calling his friends miserable comforters who make long-winded speeches. He proceeds to place responsiblity on God both for his troubles and for ending them.

JOB 15

1. a. How can a believer's doubts or questioning of God shake others' faith (verses 4–6)? _____

_____

_____

b. Would it have been better for Job to keep his feelings to himself (Rom. 14:13, 22, NIV)? Or was it better for him to express them and deal with them openly? _____

_____

_____

Note: In verses 5–6 Eliphaz says that Job's speech proves he is a great sinner. Eliphaz seems glad to have proof for his charges; however, a moment's reflection will show that Job's speech did not become vehement until his friends provoked him.

2. Job has only claimed to be as wise as his friends (12:3; 13:2), yet Eliphaz accuses him of pride and of claiming to have special insights from God (15:7–9). Does one person understand or accept God's ways better than another does? Explain. (See 1 Cor. 2:14–16.) _____

_____

_____

3. What consolations does Eliphaz refer to in verse 11?

_____

4. Summarize verses 14–35. _____

_____

_____

_____

_____

_____

JOB 16

Note: Chapters 16 and 17 are difficult for all commentators; many verses are difficult to translate.

5. Why is Job sure he would do a better job of comforting than his friends did (verses 1–5)? _____

_____

_____

6. How was Job a type of Christ, a "picture forecast" of what the Messiah would have to endure? Compare verses 9–11 with Psalm 22:6–8 and Matthew 26:67; 27:29–30, 39–44. _____

_____

_____

7. Job realizes (verses 7–14) that his suffering is *through* wicked men, but he claims God is the one who brings suffering to him even though he has not been guilty of great sin. As a committed, forgiven believer, do you believe your suffering comes from God or the Devil? Explain. _____

_____

_____

8. On whom is Job depending by faith (16:18–22)? See also Romans 8:33–34 and Hebrews 7:24–25. _____

How does that comfort you? _____

_____

JOB 17

9. What is Job talking about in verse 3? See Psalms 49:7–9; 130:7–8; Hebrews 9:13–15. _____

_____

_____

_____

Note: In verse 6 Job says he has become a "byword" or a "proverb." He may be referring to the preceding verse, saying that those words are a proverb applied to him. More likely, people were saying to one another, "Did you hear about Job?" Job is still a byword today. People speak of the patience of Job. And when someone says, "I'm walking in Job's shoes" or "I'm a Job," we know immediately that he or she is experiencing inexplicable suffering.

10. Job challenges his comforters in verse 10. What good, for Job and his friends, comes from this often sarcastic discussion? _____

_____

_____

11. When visiting a suffering person, should you discuss only safe, soothing topics? Should you tell the sufferer about other people's problems? Explain. _____

_____

_____

_____

12. Suggest some suitable topics you can talk about with someone who is terminally ill. _____

_____

_____

7

BILDAD AND ZOPHAR SPEAK AGAIN AND JOB ANSWERS

Job 18–21

In these chapters Bildad and Zophar list the agonies of the wicked, inferring that since Job is suffering agony, he must be wicked. Job bemoans his fate. He writhes under the pressure of God's hand (19:21) but still trusts Him. He points out that many wicked people live in prosperity and die honored. Since that is the case, Job says his friends speak nonsense and falsehood.

Job had said, "But come on, all of you, try again! I will not find a wise man among you" (17:10). His friends resent that challenge and respond to it in these chapters.

JOB 18

1. a. Has Bildad really listened to Job? _____

    b. How does he show he is more interested in getting his point across than in comforting Job? _____

2. Summarize Bildad's speech in one short sentence. _____

JOB 19

Note: Children often say, "Sticks and stones may break my bones, but words can never hurt me." That is a lie. The saying is usually quoted when one is suffering pain from cruel words. In verse 2 Job says he is being crushed by words, as if his friends were stoning him.

3. a. Have Job's friends exalted themselves above him (verse 5)? Do they feel more righteous because they are not suffering? _____

b. Do you ever feel that way when you think of someone who has an unusual amount of trouble? Explain. _____

4. a. Can righteousness be measured by material blessings?

b. What do you learn from Psalm 49:16–20? _____

c. Who was richer at this point, Job or his friends? _____

5. a. In verse 7 Job says God doesn't hear his prayers. Have you ever felt that way? _____

b. Does God's silence indicate that He doesn't hear us, that He is inactive or uncaring? _____

_____

_____

6. a. In verse 11 and in 16:9 Job says that his suffering comes because of God's anger (see Ps. 90:9, 11; Lam. 1:12). Hebrews 12:4—11 states that suffering is evidence of God's love. How do you suppose a sufferer would respond if you told him or her that trials are evidence of God's special love?

_____

_____

b. Does God's love in trials make them enjoyable? See Hebrews 12:11. _____

_____

c. If you do not have trials, do you feel God loves you less? Explain. _____

_____

_____

7. a. Read Job 19:13—22. What hurts Job most? _____

_____

_____

b. Why do friends and family often neglect people in mental institutions and nursing homes? _____

_____

8. a. How is Job's experience like that of the psalmists and Christ (see Job 19:13–14; Pss. 38:11; 69:20–21; 88:8; Isa. 53:3; Mark 14:50, 66–72)? _____

_____

_____

_____

b. What are some of your experiences of rejection? _____

_____

c. How does it comfort you to realize that Christ suffered in this way (Heb. 4:14–16)? _____

_____

9. Notice the dramatic change to confidence and hope in Job 19:25–29. Compare this to Psalm 31:9–16. What produces this change (Ps. 32:10; Heb. 11:1; Eph. 2:8)? _____

_____

_____

JOB 20

10. a. Compare Zophar's speech in chapter 20 with Bildad's in chapter 18. How are they alike? How are they different? _____

_____

_____

_____

b. Is Zophar's tone the same as Bildad's, or has Zophar been touched by Job's speech in chapter 19? _____

JOB 21

Notice that Job's answer is a carefully planned rebuttal of his friends' arguments. Job backs up his argument by telling his friends to ask travelers from other countries if they haven't found the same to be true in their observation (verse 29).

11. How does Job refute the following arguments?

Arguments	Job's Refutation
5:17–27	21:7–16
20:11	21:7, 13
18:19	21:8–11
18:17–18; 20:7–9	21:30–33

12. Is the tone of Job's answer to Zophar kinder than his answer to Bildad? Explain. _____

_____

_____

13. Job says his friends' comfort is empty nonsense (verse 34). Give an example of empty comfort that someone has given. _____

_____

_____

CONCLUSION

14. How does your belief in the resurrection of Christ and the resurrection of the saints in the Last Day comfort you when you have trials? Consider John 5:24–27; 11:25–26; 1 Corinthians 15:12–18. _____

_____

_____

_____

8

ELIPHAZ AND JOB EXCHANGE WORDS

Job 22–24

As we study speech after speech, with no one being persuaded to change, we wonder why God lets this go on. What profit is there in studying the same basic arguments over and over? It seems that God knows we need to learn and relearn these truths because we so easily fall into the thinking patterns held by Job's friends. We tend to believe that suffering is a punishment and that we are more righteous than those who suffer. Again and again we need to be taught the proper response to suffering, especially when it goes on for a long time.

Job 22 contains Eliphaz's last speech. His premise is wrong, but he is still trying to help his friend. First he probes for hidden sins; then he pleads with Job to submit to God, to repent, and to return to Him. Finally he pastors Job, attempting to herd this wandering sheep into the fold with assurances that there he will find peace.

JOB 22

1. How would you answer Eliphaz's questions in verses 2–3? _____

_____

_____

2. Why does Eliphaz level accusations against Job in verses 4–11? _____

_____

_____

3. a. How did these believers respond to unjust accusations?

Hannah (1 Sam. 1:14–16) _____

_____

Nehemiah (Neh. 6:5–9) _____

_____

Jeremiah (Jer. 37:12–20) _____

_____

b. How did Jesus respond to unjust accusations (Matt. 27:11–14; 1 Peter 2:19–23)? _____

_____

_____

c. How should contemporary Christians respond to slander or unjust accusations? Ignore it? Sue? Write a letter of defense? Publicize the accuser's sins? Consult Matthew 5:11–12, 44; 1 Peter 3:15–17; Proverbs 15:1; and 1 Corinthians 6:1–6. _____

_____

_____

_____

_____

4. Note the discrepancies between Eliphaz's charges in 22:12−18 and Job's words in 7:16−21. Why had Eliphaz not accepted Job's defense after his earlier accusations? _____

_____

_____

5. What does Eliphaz accuse Job of in verses 23−25? _____

_____

6. Eliphaz claims to be righteous (verse 18). Yet what should he have done according to his statement in verses 27−30? _____

_____

JOB 23

Job is bitter here, not rebellious. He is like Naomi in Ruth 1:20−21, " 'Don't call me Naomi,' she told them. 'Call me Mara, because the Almighty has made my life very bitter. I went away full, but the LORD has brought me back empty. Why call me Naomi? The LORD has afflicted me; the Almighty has brought misfortune upon me.' "

7. What is Job's assurance in verses 1−7? _____

_____

_____

Note: Verses 8−12 are a poem demonstrating that Job expects a personal relationship to God that comes only through obedience.

8. What is Job's problem in verses 8–9? _____

_____

9. What is Job's testimony in verse 10? _____

_____

10. Would it be easier for Job to bear the suffering as punishment for sin than to bear it as a test of righteousness (verses 11–12)? Explain. _____

_____

11. Consider verses 13–17. Should a Christian go through life cowering before God, expecting trial after trial from Him? What advice is given in 1 Peter 4:12–19? _____

_____

_____

_____

JOB 24

This chapter has puzzled translators. Versions differ greatly, placing the verses in different order. Some translators attribute part of the chapter to Zophar. I believe, however, that Job spoke these words, perhaps after a time lapse in which he thought about and identified with others who long for justice. Job, like all sufferers, has his ups and downs.

12. What is Job's burden in verses 1–12? _____

_____

_____

_____

13. Compare Job's description of conditions then to present-day conditions (verses 1–17). What similarities can you find? _____

_____

_____

_____

14. Verse 12 is the key verse in this passage. In our western culture many Christians move to the suburbs and become insensitive to the problems of inner-city residents. How is God at work in the inner city, and how can we assist in this work? _____

_____

_____

15. What have you learned from this lesson? _____

_____

_____

_____

9

BILDAD AND JOB EXCHANGE WORDS

Job 25–31

Bildad feels hopeless and is running out of words, but Job, after a sarcastic reply, assumes the burden of teaching his friends. "God has unstrung my bow, . . ." he says. "My harp is tuned to mourning, and my flute to the sound of wailing" (30:11, 31). Yet these chapters are a beautiful sad song, a last defense.

JOB 25

1. a. What challenge does Job fling out in 24:25? _____

_____

b. What is Bildad's response in chapter 25? _____

_____

Note: Job's reply (chapters 26–31) is not one long, unbroken speech. In chapter 26 he replies to Bildad and then describes God's power in creation. Chapter 27 presents his concluding answer to his friends' speeches and charges. Chapter 28 is a free-standing speech, which may have been given after a lapse of time. It contains Job's reflections on men's accomplishments and the search for wisdom. These thoughts prepare all the characters for God's answer given in chapters 38–41. In Job's last speech (chapters 29–31) he reflects on his past happiness, bemoans his present misery, and presents his last defense.

JOB 26

2. Is Job's sarcasm (verses 1–4) a just response to Bildad's words in chapter 25? Explain. _____

_____

_____

3. In verses 5–14 Job describes the scope of the universe—from death to heaven—as he understands it. He says that as far as our minds can stretch, we can only take in the mere fringe of God's power and greatness. Bildad and Job agree on God's greatness as Creator. How do they differ in their conclusions about God's regard for man? Compare 25:6 with 10:8–12; 14:15–17; 19:25–27; 23:10. _____

_____

_____

_____

JOB 27

4. Job is very personal here; he hurts. He begins with an oath, calling on God to witness the truth of his claim to innocence. Job depends *by faith* on God for justification, yet he says that God has denied him justice (verse 2). *Does the* *just God ever deny justice?* Consider the cases of innocent people who suffer and die in prison, falsely accused. Or think of the thousands who are or have been martyrs for their faith.

_____

_____

5. Read verses 5—6. Is Job maintaining that he has no sin or that he has not sinned greatly enough to deserve this punishment? Compare to David (Pss. 26 and 51) and Paul (Acts 9:1—5 and 1 Cor. 4:4). _____

_____

_____

6. Job, who has suffered loss of almost everything, maintains his righteousness. In verses 7—23 he describes the ultimate end of the wicked—they lose everything. Is he comparing or contrasting himself to the wicked? Explain.

_____

_____

JOB 28

This chapter is an interlude. It is calm and thoughtful and provides a transition between the dialogue and the monologues that follow. It points out the need for God's wisdom. All of the characters in this book are exhausted. They need God's wisdom. Verses 12 and 20 are the key verses.

7. What does Job describe in verses 1—11? _____

_____

_____

8. What is the message of verses 13—19? _____

_____

_____

9. a. In Proverbs 4:7 we read, "Wisdom is supreme; therefore get wisdom. Though it cost all you have, get understanding." How can we get wisdom (James 1:5–6)?

_____

b. What evidence proves that a person has wisdom and understanding (James 3:13, 17)? _____

_____

c. Did Job's life provide evidence of such wisdom and understanding (chapters 29 and 31)? _____

_____

10. What comfort does Job find in verses 20–28? _____

_____

Note: Job's final speech is divided into three parts: chapter 29, a nostalgic look at the happy past; chapter 30, a piteous description of the miseries of the present; chapter 31, a presentation of all the evidence for his final plea of "not guilty." This monologue is spoken to God and himself.

JOB 29

11. Describe Job's status from the information in this chapter. _____

_____

12. a. According to verses 18–20 what did Job assume about his life? _____

_____

b. Do you assume the same about your life? _____

_____

JOB 30

This chapter is an extreme contrast to the preceding one. God gave, but He also took away. Notice the word "now" in verses 1, 9, 11, and 16 which contrast the present to the past.

13. What group of people is Job talking about in verses 1–14? _____

_____

14. a. In verse 15 Job speaks of the loss of dignity that comes with illness or suffering. Today we see the same loss of dignity in people who are unemployed, divorced, handicapped, mentally ill, rejected by family or friends, or convicted of breaking the law. What is dignity? _____

_____

b. How can we help suffering people keep their dignity?

_____

_____

JOB 31

In this chapter Job pleads "not guilty"—with oaths! He says, "If I have done _____, then let _____ happen to me. I'll take any punishment I deserve!"

15. List the sins of which Job claims he is not guilty:

1–4 _____

5–8 _____

9–12 _____

13–15 _____

16–23 _____

24–28 _____

29–30 _____

31–32 _____

33–34 _____

38–40 _____

16. a. What reasons does Job give in verses 14 and 23 for living a godly life? _____

_____

b. Are these good reasons for serving God? _____

What would you add? _____

_____

_____

17. Is it right or helpful to plead with God, reminding Him of our good deeds? Discuss this after reading Psalm 26, Psalm 41:1–3, Matthew 6:1–4, and Luke 17:7–10. _____

_____

_____

_____

CONCLUSION

Job signs off in verses 35–37 (verses 38–40 are a postscript). He ends his defense and asks that his accusation be put in writing. Job is confident he will be proven right—he has an answer for every question.

10

ELIHU GIVES YOUTHFUL ADVICE

Job 32–37

When we began the study of Job, we saw a blameless, upright man cast into sorrow and stricken with pain and suffering. His three friends, Eliphaz, Bildad, and Zophar came to him as he sat in the city dump—a piece of human refuse. After a week of silence, these friends began a long discussion with Job, attempting to find the reason for his suffering.

How long did this take? We don't know. It may have been weeks with days passing between speeches, or it may have been days with hours passing between speeches.

Was Job alone with his friends? Evidently not. In Job 17:6 we read that Job became a byword; everyone was talking about him. People—adults, children, even criminals—came to look at him (16:10; 30:1, 9–10). And all the while one young man looked on and listened.

Elihu was not mentioned in the introduction of Job's

friends (2:11). He breaks into the action, claiming to have listened patiently to all the other speeches, and now he offers his solution to the problem. He is never heard from again— even God does not mention him in the epilogue (42:7–9).

Though scholars cannot agree how Elihu's speeches fit into the book, his speeches present a youthful approach to Job's problem. Elihu often contradicts himself and generally agrees with the other three friends. But he tries to help. He begins his speech respectfully and introduces a new thought trend.

JOB 32

1. a. Why did Elihu become angry at Job for failing to justify God? _____

_____

b. Would you become angry if you visited a sufferer and he or she said that God was not being fair? _____

c. How would you reply? _____

2. a. Do you agree that young people as well as old people can speak wisely? How is their approach different? _____

b. How should young people go about giving advice to older people? Consider 1 Timothy 4:11–12; 5:1–2. _____

_____

_____

c. Which of these standards does Elihu measure up to?

_____

3. What do you learn about Elihu's character from chapters 32–33? _____

JOB 33

4. Describe Elihu's way of speaking (32:17–33:13, 31–33). _____

5. In Job 33:8–9 Elihu says that he has heard Job claim to be sinless. Read 7:21; 9:15, 20; 10:6; and 14:6–17. Is Elihu quoting Job correctly? Explain. _____

6. What does Elihu see as the purpose of suffering (33:14–30; 36:8–12)? _____

JOB 34

This begins Elihu's second speech. In his time and culture, words were the primary art form (verse 3). In this speech Elihu shows off his skill with words. He is interested no longer in helping Job, but in scoring debate points. He is less personal. Elihu defends God's justice (34:10–17). He recognizes God's authority (34:18–20).

7. What does Elihu accuse Job of in verses 31–37? _____

8. Elihu says that Job should suffer even more because he has spoken against God (verse 36). How would you reply to Elihu if you were present? _____

JOB 35

This is Elihu's third speech. In it he takes Job's words and twists them. He states that Job has said, "It doesn't pay to serve God." Then he goes on to assume that Job would say, "Why not just go ahead and sin—what would it matter?" Elihu attempts to answer these questions. He then suggests that Job is asking, "Why doesn't God answer prayer?" (verse 9). He answers by saying God doesn't hear the prayers of sinful people (verses 13 and 16). He implies that God will not answer Job because his prayers are sinful—arrogant, empty talk.

9. What kind of God does Elihu portray in chapter 35?

_____

_____

JOB 36:1–21

Perhaps some time passes between Elihu's third and fourth speeches. Maybe his portrayal of God as uncaring was challenged or he has reconsidered his words. At any rate, this speech has a softer tone. In it he presents God as interested in men, wanting to teach them through affliction. He suggests that the meaning of suffering depends on how it is received.

10. What do you think of Elihu's words in verses 1–4? Compare them with 37:16. _____

_____

_____

11. a. In verses 8–21 does Elihu see suffering as mercy, punishment, or both? Explain. _____

_____

_____

b. Is Elihu just in his charges against Job in verses 13–21? _____

JOB 36:22–37:24

Elihu's last speech picks up his first theme—God's greatness (33:12). The questions in 36:22–23 and the description of God's power in nature provide a transition; they prepare us for God's reply in chapters 38–41. The emphasis begins to shift from a discussion of God's justice to a description of His power and wisdom. The proper response to these is suggested in 36:24–25: Praise God, get down on your knees before Him!

12. How do Elihu's words in 36:26 and 37:5 contradict his speeches? _____

13. What dual purpose may God have in sending storms (36:31; 37:13)? _____

14. In citing this dual purpose and concluding his speech with a reminder of God's justice and greatness (verse 23), how is Elihu wiser than Eliphaz, Bildad, and Zophar? _____

CONCLUSION

Four friends have spoken to Job, and we have listened and learned. We sigh, wishing someone would say an encouraging word to him. Let us call on David, who also suffered, to minister to Job and other sufferers with the words of Psalm 37:1–11.

Do not fret because of evil men
*   or be envious of those who do wrong;*
for like the grass they will soon wither,
*   like green plants they will soon die away.*

Trust in the LORD *and do good;*
*   dwell in the land and enjoy safe pasture.*
Delight yourself in the LORD
*   and he will give you the desires of your heart.*

Commit your way to the LORD;
*   trust in him and he will do this:*
He will make your righteousness shine like the
*   dawn,*
*   the justice of your cause like the noonday sun.*

Be still before the LORD *and wait patiently for him;*
*   do not fret when men succeed in their ways,*
*   when they carry out their wicked schemes.*

Refrain from anger and turn from wrath;
*   do not fret—it leads only to evil.*
For evil men will be cut off,
*   but those who hope in the* LORD *will inherit the*
*   land.*

A little while, and the wicked will be no more;
*   though you look for them, they will not be*
*   found.*
But the meek will inherit the land
*   and enjoy great peace.*

11

GOD SPEAKS

Job 38–39

God has heard all that has been said. A tremendous storm hushes the men and gets their attention. God speaks in the storm.

JOB 38

1. To whom does God speak (verse 1)? _____

_____

2. a. Does God accuse Job of sin in verse 2? _____

   b. Is ignorance a sin? _____

3. What is the tone of God's words in chapters 38 and 39? Angry? Loving? Sarcastic? Gentle? Reassuring? Chiding? Comforting? _____

_____

4. Find at least fifteen created things God refers to in this first speech (chapters 38 and 39). _____

_____

_____

_____

5. a. God brings Job's attention to nature. What do we learn about God from nature (Ps. 19:1–6)? _____

_____

b. What should be the response of anyone who seriously considers the marvels of nature (Rom. 1:18–23—especially verse 21)? _____

_____

6. a. Read Job 38:22–23. How did God use weather in Judges 4–5 and 1 Samuel 7:10? _____

_____

b. Can you think of any examples of this from modern history? _____

_____

7. Read Job 38:22–30, 34–38. How does God use weather to control people's lives? _____

_____

8. Read Job 38:31–33. How do natural laws and the study of astronomy affect mankind? _____

_____

9. What specific things do we learn about God in Job 38:39–41? See also Psalm 34:10. _____

_____

JOB 39

10. What do we learn about God in verses 1–4? See Psalm 139:13–16. _____

_____

_____

11. Job's agony was caused by God's silence, rejection, or abandonment (13:24; 19:7; 23:3–5; 29:2–5). When God does speak and question Job, does it comfort him? _____

12. a. Look back over the questions God asks in these chapters. Suppose God addressed these questions to you. What effect would they have on you? _____

_____

b. What difference should or would that make in your life? _____

_____

13. What in God's creation inspires you to praise Him?

_____

_____

12

GOD CONTINUES

Job 40–41

The storm ceases, and Job is left speechless. He has no answer to God's questions; he can only marvel at God's greatness. Again God speaks to him out of a storm.

JOB 40

1. What is Job's reaction to God's questioning? _____

_____

2. What stance does Job take toward sin in his life? _____

_____

_____

3. Does God accuse Job of sin in verse 8? _____

4. What does God want Job to admit in verses 9–14? _____

_____

Note: God now uses two examples from nature to instruct Job: the behemoth, the fiercest land creature; and the leviathan, a terrifying sea monster. Some people think these are mythical monsters, but 40:15 points out that they are created beings as was Job. God uses extravagant poetical picture language to describe the behemoth, which seems much like the hippopotamus, except for the tail (verse 17). Many translators believe the word 'tail' in verse 17 should be translated 'trunk': God may be describing here an elephant and his marvelous trunk. Many point out that our understanding of the power of these creatures is limited because we see this type of animal only in captivity.

5. What truth does God point out to Job through the example of the behemoth in verses 15 and 19? _____

_____

JOB 41

6. a. God's last example is the leviathan, a dragon-like crocodile or sea monster. In view of who instigated Job's testing, whom could the leviathan symbolize? Read Isaiah 27:1 and Revelation 12:7–9. _____

_____

b. Only who can control the power of Satan, the accuser (Rev. 12:10–12)? _____

7. a. What is God forcing Job to acknowledge in verses 10–11? _____

_____

b. What comfort does this give Job? _____

_____

8. After studying chapters 38–41, why do you think God replied to Job with these questions? Choose one or more of these responses and explain your choice:

a. To shrink Job's opinion of himself. _____

_____

b. To show the proportion of man's knowledge to God's knowledge. _____

_____

c. To point out Job's sin. _____

_____

d. To teach Job about God. _____

_____

e. To get Job to trust God's power. _____

_____

f. To test Job's knowledge. _____

_____

g. To rebuild Job's faith. _____

_____

h. To reassure Job that all would turn out well. _____

_____

9. Job learned to know God better, but he did not learn the purpose of his severe test. Which would be more comforting to you—to know God's reasons for everything or to know God and His power? Why? _____

_____

_____

_____

10. After studying these forty-one chapters, how will your approach in comforting sufferers change? _____

_____

_____

11. a. God's people throughout the centuries have obeyed and suffered, often not knowing why or not seeing any good come from their suffering. What sustained them? Read Hebrews 11. _____

_____

_____

b. Were they rewarded? How? _____

_____

c. What sustains you in trials? _____

_____

d. As you look into the unknown future, do you feel helpless or hopeful? Explain. _____

_____

13

JOB IS RESTORED

Job 42

Job's prayer was heard. God answered him. One can feel the quietness, the peace as Job relaxes, no longer feeling rejected by God. Job lives once again in the light of God's smile.

JOB 42

1. What comfort did Job find in God's words to him? _____

_____

2. What sins did Job confess and repent of (verses 1–6)?

_____

_____

3. Who won the contest between God and Satan (2:4–6)?

_____

Note: Job says, "My ears had heard of you but now my eyes have seen you" (42:5). He had learned more about himself and God. He had learned to compare himself with God, which prompted him to say, "God be merciful to me, a sinner!"

Pride, wealth, social status, job security, education, independence can keep us from making this humble confession. Job lost everything, and in that experience he received a personal knowledge of God. We should examine our own relationships to God and ask, "Do we truly know Him, or have we only heard about Him?"

4. God said that Job had spoken what was right. Does this mean that it was right for Job to question God, to accuse Him of injustice, to remind God of his righteous life? Give reasons for your answer. _____

_____

_____

5. Job—the wronged one, the sufferer—prayed for his accusers. Compare him to

a. Moses (Num. 12) _____

_____

b. Jesus (Luke 23:34) _____

_____

c. Stephen (Acts 7:54–60) _____

_____

Why did God insist that Job pray for his friends? _____

_____

What effect does such prayer have on the sufferer who prays? _____

_____

6. Job's friends and family—who had rejected him in his suffering—celebrated with him, gave gifts, and comforted him *after* he was healed and made prosperous. What does this teach you? _____

_____

_____

7. Why was the latter part of Job's life more blessed than the former (verses 12–15)? _____

_____

Note: Job's daughters, not his sons, are named in verses 14–15. Their father gave them an inheritance equal to that of their brothers, something not often done in that male-dominated culture. This blameless servant of God was progressive and practiced sexual equality.

8. What can you learn from verses 16 and 17? _____

_____

Note: Many people want to know if Job had the same wife after he was restored. We don't know, but since we are not told of a new wife, we assume he had the same one. Some people also want to know how old Job was when his troubles began and how long they lasted. We don't know. Some believe that since God doubled things in Job's restoration, the added 140 years of life may have been double his age (seventy) at the time the troubles began. By seventy he certainly could have had grown children, many possessions, and great prestige.

9. If Job could have selected a psalm (or part of one) to express his thoughts after all these experiences, which one do you think he would have chosen? Why? _____

10. Does God say to us in this book that if we endure as Job did and do not curse God, we will be restored and receive double in this life? Explain. _____

_____

_____

11. Why does God include this book in the Bible? _____

_____

12. How is your life richer for having studied Job? _____

_____

_____

CONCLUSION

In this study we have met Job, several psalmists, other Bible characters, and some of our contemporaries who have suffered or are suffering. We have learned to be more thankful for our Lord Jesus, who suffered for us so that we may be restored in mercy and love to fellowship with God.

By grace and through faith each believer can say, even when sitting on the ash heap of suffering:

I know that my Redeemer lives,
and that in the end he will stand upon the
earth.
And after my skin has been destroyed,
yet in my flesh I will see God;
I myself will see him
with my own eyes—I, and not another.
How my heart yearns within me!

Job 19:25−27

BIBLIOGRAPHY

Anderson, Francis I. *Job, An Introduction and Commentary.* London: Tyndale Press, 1976.

Barabas, Steven. "Job," *The Zondervan Pictorial Encyclopedia of the Bible.* Grand Rapids, Michigan: Zondervan Publishing House, 1975.

Brand, Paul and Philip Yancey. *In His Image.* Grand Rapids, Michigan: Zondervan Publishing House, 1984.

Eppinga, Jacob. Sermon on Job 42, La Grave Avenue Christian Reformed Church, Grand Rapids, Michigan, February 19, 1984.

Fuller, George C. *Personal Suffering: Sermons on Job.* Philadelphia: Westminster Media, Westminster Theological Seminary, 1980.

Smedes, Lewis B. *How Can It Be All Right When Everything Is All Wrong?* San Francisco: Harper & Row Publishers, 1982.

Yancey, Philip. *Where Is God When It Hurts?* Grand Rapids, Michigan: Zondervan Publishing House, 1977.

Youngblood, Ronald. *Old Testament Overview, Tape 25.* Wheaton, Illinois: Wheaton College Graduate School Extension Studies.